Considerations on the slave trade; and the consumption of West Indian produce.

Thomas Cooper

Gale ECCO Print Editions

Relive history with *Eighteenth Century Collections Online*, now available in print for the independent historian and collector. This series includes the most significant English-language and foreign-language works printed in Great Britain during the eighteenth century, and is organized in seven different subject areas including literature and language; medicine, science, and technology; and religion and philosophy. The collection also includes thousands of important works from the Americas.

The eighteenth century has been called "The Age of Enlightenment." It was a period of rapid advance in print culture and publishing, in world exploration, and in the rapid growth of science and technology – all of which had a profound impact on the political and cultural landscape. At the end of the century the American Revolution, French Revolution and Industrial Revolution, perhaps three of the most significant events in modern history, set in motion developments that eventually dominated world political, economic, and social life.

In a groundbreaking effort, Gale initiated a revolution of its own: digitization of epic proportions to preserve these invaluable works in the largest online archive of its kind. Contributions from major world libraries constitute over 175,000 original printed works. Scanned images of the actual pages, rather than transcriptions, recreate the works *as they first appeared.*

Now for the first time, these high-quality digital scans of original works are available via print-on-demand, making them readily accessible to libraries, students, independent scholars, and readers of all ages.

For our initial release we have created seven robust collections to form one the world's most comprehensive catalogs of 18th century works.

Initial Gale ECCO Print Editions collections include:

History and Geography
Rich in titles on English life and social history, this collection spans the world as it was known to eighteenth-century historians and explorers. Titles include a wealth of travel accounts and diaries, histories of nations from throughout the world, and maps and charts of a world that was still being discovered. Students of the War of American Independence will find fascinating accounts from the British side of conflict.

Social Science

Delve into what it was like to live during the eighteenth century by reading the first-hand accounts of everyday people, including city dwellers and farmers, businessmen and bankers, artisans and merchants, artists and their patrons, politicians and their constituents. Original texts make the American, French, and Industrial revolutions vividly contemporary.

Medicine, Science and Technology

Medical theory and practice of the 1700s developed rapidly, as is evidenced by the extensive collection, which includes descriptions of diseases, their conditions, and treatments. Books on science and technology, agriculture, military technology, natural philosophy, even cookbooks, are all contained here.

Literature and Language

Western literary study flows out of eighteenth-century works by Alexander Pope, Daniel Defoe, Henry Fielding, Frances Burney, Denis Diderot, Johann Gottfried Herder, Johann Wolfgang von Goethe, and others. Experience the birth of the modern novel, or compare the development of language using dictionaries and grammar discourses.

Religion and Philosophy

The Age of Enlightenment profoundly enriched religious and philosophical understanding and continues to influence present-day thinking. Works collected here include masterpieces by David Hume, Immanuel Kant, and Jean-Jacques Rousseau, as well as religious sermons and moral debates on the issues of the day, such as the slave trade. The Age of Reason saw conflict between Protestantism and Catholicism transformed into one between faith and logic -- a debate that continues in the twenty-first century.

Law and Reference

This collection reveals the history of English common law and Empire law in a vastly changing world of British expansion. Dominating the legal field is the *Commentaries of the Law of England* by Sir William Blackstone, which first appeared in 1765. Reference works such as almanacs and catalogues continue to educate us by revealing the day-to-day workings of society.

Fine Arts

The eighteenth-century fascination with Greek and Roman antiquity followed the systematic excavation of the ruins at Pompeii and Herculaneum in southern Italy; and after 1750 a neoclassical style dominated all artistic fields. The titles here trace developments in mostly English-language works on painting, sculpture, architecture, music, theater, and other disciplines. Instructional works on musical instruments, catalogs of art objects, comic operas, and more are also included.

The BiblioLife Network

This project was made possible in part by the BiblioLife Network (BLN), a project aimed at addressing some of the huge challenges facing book preservationists around the world. The BLN includes libraries, library networks, archives, subject matter experts, online communities and library service providers. We believe every book ever published should be available as a high-quality print reproduction; printed on-demand anywhere in the world. This insures the ongoing accessibility of the content and helps generate sustainable revenue for the libraries and organizations that work to preserve these important materials.

The following book is in the "public domain" and represents an authentic reproduction of the text as printed by the original publisher. While we have attempted to accurately maintain the integrity of the original work, there are sometimes problems with the original work or the micro-film from which the books were digitized. This can result in minor errors in reproduction. Possible imperfections include missing and blurred pages, poor pictures, markings and other reproduction issues beyond our control. Because this work is culturally important, we have made it available as part of our commitment to protecting, preserving, and promoting the world's literature.

GUIDE TO FOLD-OUTS MAPS and OVERSIZED IMAGES

The book you are reading was digitized from microfilm captured over the past thirty to forty years. Years after the creation of the original microfilm, the book was converted to digital files and made available in an online database.

In an online database, page images do not need to conform to the size restrictions found in a printed book. When converting these images back into a printed bound book, the page sizes are standardized in ways that maintain the detail of the original. For large images, such as fold-out maps, the original page image is split into two or more pages

Guidelines used to determine how to split the page image follows:

• Some images are split vertically; large images require vertical and horizontal splits.
• For horizontal splits, the content is split left to right.
• For vertical splits, the content is split from top to bottom.
• For both vertical and horizontal splits, the image is processed from top left to bottom right.

CONSIDERATIONS

ON

K Cooper (?)

THE SLAVE TRADE;

AND THE

CONSUMPTION

OF

WEST INDIAN PRODUCE.

————————

London:

Printed and fold by DARTON and HARVEY, Gracechurch-Street;
J. CARTER, back of the Royal Exchange, and J. PARSONS,
Paternofter Row.

[Price 1d. or 6s per Hundred, to thofe who give them away.]

————

MDCCXCI.

On the First of January, 1792,
is intended to be published,

A N

EPISTLE

T O

W. WILBERFORCE, ESQ.

A POEM:

Written during the late Disturbances in the
WEST INDIES.

Printed and sold by DARTON and HARVEY, No. 55,
Gracechurch-street. Price 6d.

———

Where also may be had,

Price 1d or 5s. per Hundred to those who give them away,

REMARKABLE EXTRACTS

RELATING TO THE

SLAVE TRADE;

From the Writings of various Authors.

TO THE READER.

THE fubftance of the following paper is extracted from " Letters on the Slave Trade," by T. Cooper, Efq. and the obligation to abftain from the confumption of Weft Indian produce, infifted upon at the end, has already been laid before the public, in an Addrefs to the Inhabitants of Great Britain, by an anonymous writer. This is printed by a Society, which, had it's funds been adequate to the expence, would rather have republifhed thofe two excellent pamphlets; it is hoped, however, that fufficient will be found here to fatisfy every thoughtful and unbiaffed perfon.

Hackney,
October 8, 1791.

ADVERTISEMENT.

————————————

THE confumption of Sugar in this country is fo immenfe, that the quantity commonly ufed by individuals will have an important effect. A family that ufes five pounds of Sugar *per week*, with the fame proportion of Rum, will, by abftaining from the confumption 21 months, prevent the flavery, or murder, of one fellow creature; eight fuch families in nineteen years and a half, would prevent the flavery, or murder, of 100, and 38,000 would totally prevent the Slave Trade, by removing the occafion to fupply our iflands.—A French writer obferves, " That he cannot look upon a piece of Sugar without conceiving it ftained with fpots of human blood." and Dr. Franklin very, properly adds, " That had he taken in all the confequences, he might have feen the Sugar not merely fpotted, but dyed fcarlet in grain."

Vide An Addrefs to the People of Great Britain, on the Utility of refraining from Weft Indian Sugar and Rum. Edition 5, page 4. fold by Gurney, Holborn and Darton, and Co. Gracechurch-Street, 1791.

CONSIDERATIONS

ON THE

SLAVE TRADE.

———————————

THE iniquity of the African Slave Trade is fo glaring that it has met with fcarcely any but anonymous defenders, while thofe who oppofe it have openly publifhed their names, and defied all the patrons of this barbarous traffic, either to contradict their facts, or invalidate their arguments. This is a ftrong prefumption in favour of their caufe, fince no man of character would publicly atteft what he had not the beft reafon to think was true; and, on the other hand, the moft depraved mind would not quietly endure the charge of injuftice and cruelty, if it were not confcious of an inability to refute it. The African merchants and Weft India planters, are a numerous body of men, they have been accufed of crimes at which human nature fhudders, of rapine, torture, murder, in the moft varied and horrid forms. The charge has now been for fome years before the public; they have the beft opportunities of collecting information, and have had abundant time to difprove it, and yet not one of them has attempted even to alleviate, to glofs over, the iniquity of their proceedings. What ftronger proof can we have that the charge is founded? Silence in this cafe, is a confeffion of guilt; for thefe men muft be well acquainted with the fubject, and, having the ftrongeft motives, would long ago have repelled the charge if they poffibly could.

B

The facts, therefore, which Benezet, Wesley, Clarkson, and various other writers on this interesting subject have produced, may be regarded as undoubtedly true; and as they need only be generally known, to excite general abhorrence of the trade, and zeal for it's abolition, a few of the most striking are here selected, and earnestly recommended to attention. An account is first given of the means of procuring slaves, then of the method of conveying them from the coast of Africa, to the West India Islands; and lastly, of the treatment they meet with there.

To explain the manner in which negro slaves are procured, it will suffice to give an extract of two voyages to Guinea on that account. The first is taken verbatim, from the original manuscript of the surgeon's journal —" Seftro, Dec. 9. 1724. No trade to day, though many traders came on board. They informed us that the people are gone to war within land, and will bring prisoners enough in two or three days, in hopes of which we stay.—— 30th. No trade yet; but our traders came on board to day, and informed us the people had *burnt four towns*; so that to-morrow we expect slaves off.—31st. Fair weather, but no trading yet. *We see each night towns burning*, but we hear many of the Seftro men are killed by the inland negroes, so that we fear this war will be unsuccessful —Jan. 2. Last night we saw a prodigious fire break out about 11 o'clock; and this morning see the *the town of Seftro burnt down to the ground*, (it contained about 100 houses) so that we find their enemies are too hard for them at present, and consequently *our trade spoiled here*."

The second extract taken from the journal of a surgeon, who went from New York on the same trade, is as follows—The commander of the vessel sent to acquaint the king that he wanted a cargo of Slaves. The king promised to furnish him, and in order to it, set out, *designing to surprise some town and make all the people prisoners*. Some time after, the king sent him word that he had not met with the desired success, having attempted to break up two towns, and having been twice repulsed; but that he still hoped to procure the number of slaves. In this design he persisted till he met his enemies in the field. A battle was fought which lasted three days, and the engagement was fo bloody that *four thoufand five hundred men* were flain upon the fpot."—" Such is the manner wherein the negroes are procured; and thus *Chriftians* preach the gofpel to the *heathens!* exclaims the Rev. John Wefley, from whofe thoughts on flavery the preceding extracts are made. —The facts are from Benezet." *Cooper,* p. 10.

Monfieur Barbot, a French factor, fays—" Many of the flaves fold by the negroes are prifoners of war, or taken in the incurfions they make in the enemies' territories; others are ftolen. *Abundance* of little blacks of both fexes are *ftolen* away by their neighbours, when found abroad on the road, or in the woods, or elfe in the corn fields, at the time of the year when their parents keep them there all day to fcare away the devouring birds!!" *Cooper,* p. 9.

Hence we may eftimate thofe pretences, that *none* but *convicts* fentenced to death, or *prifoners* taken in war, are purchafed for flaves. Were it indeed true that none but fuch were expofed to fale, a confcientious trader could hardly buy them, till convinced that the fentence or the war was juft, the contrary to which might fairly be prefumed, fince all the African governments are defpotic, and the traffic is fo lucrative, that an avaricious and powerful prince would often be tempted *unjuftly* to condemn his fubjects, and attack his neighbours*. Indeed, " throughout the coaft where Europeans traffic, every crime, every mifdemeanour, nay, every fufpicion or crime, is made capital," and of the nature of their wars fome judgment may be formed from what has been related above.

" When flaves, thus righteoufly purchafed, are brought down to the fhips, they are examined male and female, ftark naked, by the furgeons of the veffels. Thofe who are picked out for fale, are immediately branded on the breaft (with a red hot iron which lies ready in the fire for that purpofe) with the arms and names of the company, or owners, who are the purchafers. This humane piece of caution being performed, the

---

* It is univerfally acknowledged that free perfons are fold for real or *imputed* crimes, *for the benefit of their judges.* Abftract of Evidence on the Slave Trade, p 2.

flaves are thurft by hundreds, males and females, promifcuoufly, into the the fhip*. To fay nothing of the indecency of this practice, or of the unreftrained commerce of the failors with the female flaves during the voyage, circumftances which are like the fmall duft in the balance of iniquity, the mifery of a fituation fo extremely confined, the peftilential vapours they inhale, the badnefs of the provifions on which they are fed, the fmall quantity allowed them, and the tortures of a fultry climate, are frequently fo great, that many flaves have been known to ftarve themfelves to death on the voyage, others, when brought upon deck for frefh air, have fprung overboard, to meet death in the waves; or have otherwife put an end to an exiftence fo miferable, as to make a deliverance from it the greateft bleffing they are capable of receiving." *Cooper.* p. 13.

Benezet relates a circumftance, from a perfon of undoubted credit, who heard it from the captain's own mouth. Upon an enquiry what had been the fuccefs of his voyage, he anfwered, " That he found it a difficult matter *to fet the negroes a fighting* with each other, in order to procure the number he wanted, but that when he had obtained this end, and got his veffel filled with flaves, a new difficulty arofe from their refufal to take food, thofe defperate creatures choofing to die with hunger rather than be carried from their native country " Upon a further enquiry by what means he had prevailed upon them to forego that defperate refolution, he anfwered, ' That he obliged all the negroes to come upon deck, where they perfifted in their refolution of not taking food; he caufed his failors to lay hold upon one of the moft obftinate, and chopt the poor creature into fmall pieces,

* N B Since the above was written the author has been informed that, by the late regulation the male and female flaves are not *ftowed together*, and he believes, wantonly maiming or murdering a flave, is punifhable with death, but then, as the evidence of a black is never admitted any evil-difpofed manager, may ftill be guilty of thofe crimes with impunity. An authentic ftatement of the treatment of the flaves, &c. may be found, in an Abftract of the Evidence laid before the Houfe of Commons, by the Petitioners for the Abolition of the Slave Trade. Sold by J Phillips George-Yard, Lombard-Street, and Darton and Harvey, No 55, Gracechurch Street.

forcing fome of the others to eat a part of the manggled body, withal fwearing to the furvivors,' that he would ufe them all, one after another, in the fame manner, if they did not confent to eat. This horrid execution he applauded as a good act, it having had the defired effect in bringing them to take food." *Cooper*, p. 14.

" When the fhip arrives at it's deftined port, the flaves are once more expofed to fale Here they are again 'fubjected to the infpection of other brutal *receivers*, who examine and treat them with an inhumanity at which even avarice would blufh. To this mortifying circumftance is added another—that they are picked out, as the purchafer pleafes, without any confideration whether the wife is feparated from her hufband, or the mother from her fon; and if thefe cruel inftances of feparation fhould happen; if relations, when they find themfelves about to be parted, fhould cling together, if filial, conjugal, or parental affection fhould detain them but a moment longer in each others' arms than their *fecond receivers* fhould think fit, the *lafh* inftantly fevers them from their embraces.

" When the wretched Africans are conveyed to the plantations, they are confidered as *beafts of labour*, and are put to their refpective work. Having led in their own country a life of indolence and eafe, where the earth brings forth fpontaneoufly the comforts of life, and fpares frequently the toil and trouble of cultivation, they can hardly be expected to endure the drudgeries of fervitude. Calculations are accordingly made upon their lives. It is conjectured, that if three in four furvive the *feafoning*, the bargain is highly favourable. This feafoning is faid to expire when the two firft years of their fervitude are compleated. It is the time which an African muft take to be fo accuftomed to the colony, as to be able to endure the common labour of a plantation, and to be put in the gang. At this period they are confidered as real and fubftantial fupplies From this period, therefore, we fhall defcribe their fituation, They are fummoned at five in the morning to begin their work, the work may be divided into two kinds, the culture of the fields, and the collection of grafs for the cattle. The laft is the moft laborious and intolerable employment, as the grafs can only be collected blade by blade, and it is to be fetched frequently twice a day, at a confiderable diftance from the plantation. In thefe two occupations they are jointly taken up, with no other intermiffion, than that of taking their fubfiftence twice, till nine at night. They then feparate for their refpective huts, when they gather fticks, prepare their fupper, and attend their families. This employs them till midnight, when they go to reft. Such is their daily way of life for rather more than half the year. They are 16 hours, including two intervals at meals, in the fervice of their mafters—they are imployed three hours afterwards in their own neceffary concerns—five only remain for fleep, and the day is finifhed. *Coop. r p 16, and 17.*

During the remainder of the year, the gang is divided into two or three bodies, and one of thefe *(befides performing the ordinary labour of the day,* is obliged to attend the mills, through the night. Thus at this time their fleep, upon a moderate computation, is reduced to three hours and a half each night. Thofe who refift the drowfinefs, which is continually coming upon them, are foon worn out, thofe who feed the mill between fleep and wake, frequently fuffer for thus obeying the calls of nature, the lofs of a hand or arm. And food and cloathing are as fparingly allowed them as fleep.

But they are not only denied a fufficient portion of reft and food, in addition to this they are haraffed with the unrelenting feverity of barbarous officers and tafk-mafters. "I do affirm, fays Captain J Smith, that I have feen the moft cruel treatment made ufe of at feveral of the Weft India iflands, particularly at Antigua. While ferving on that ftation 10 years ago, I vifited feveral of the plantations there, in confequence of meeting with an old fchool-fellow who managed an eftate in that ifland. I was introduced to one of that defcription, and too often has my heart aked to fee the cruel punifhment inflicted by the manager with fuch unconcern, as not to break in upon his jocularity.—— A poor negro is laid ftretched flat on his face on the ground, at his peril not to ftir an inch till the punifhment is over, that is in-flicted with a whip whofe thong, at the thickeft part is the fize of a man's thumb, and tapering longer than a coachman's whip. At every stroke a piece was taken out by the particular jerk of the whip, which the manager (sometimes his wife) takes care to direct. This I have *often* seen for not getting a sufficient quantity of grafs for the manager (for I well know that more goes to his fhare then the mafters) and many fuch trifling things." *Cooper*, p 22.

This is the common mode of punifhment, but it is varied at the difcretion of the manager, who, if he choofe it, may with impunity practife the moft wanton barbarity. " An iron coffin with holes in it was kept by a certain colonift as an auxiliary to the lafh In this the poor victim of the mafter's refentment was enclofed, and placed fufficiently near a fire to occafion extreme pain, and confequently fhreeks and groans, until the revenge of the mafter was fatiated "—" For rebellion (i.e. afferting their native liberty, which they have as much a right to as the air they breathe) they faften them down to the ground with crooked fticks on every limb, and then applying fire by degrees to the feet and hands, burn them gradually upwards to the head !" *Coop*, p 19.

As a fpecimen of the laws of the colonies, which fome have fondly imagined, calculated to prevent all cruelty and oppreffion, read the following

The law of Barbadoes decrees, " That if any negro under punifhment by his mafter or his order, for running away, or any other mifdemeanour, *fhall fuffer in life or member, no perfon whatever fhall be liable to any fine therefor* But if any man of *wantonnefs*, or *bloody-mindednefs*, or *cruel intention*, wilfully kill a negro of his own (now mark the fevere punifhment) he fhall pay into the public treafury, 15l. fterling and not be liable to any other punifhment or forfeiture for the fame. Act 39.

Nearly allied to this is the law of Virginia—" After proclamation is iffued againft flaves that run away, it is lawful for any perfons whatever to kill and deftoy fuch flaves, *by fuch ways and means as he fhall think fit* '

" We have already feen fome of the ways and means, which have been *thought fit* on fuch occafions, and many more might be mentioned. *One gentleman, whilst I was abroad, thought fit to roast his slave alive!* but if the moſt natural act of running away from intolerable tyranny, deſerves ſuch relentleſs ſeverity, what puniſhment have theſe *law makers* to expect hereafter, on account of their own enormous offences ?"

" This is the plain, unaggravated matter of fact. Such is the manner wherein our African ſlaves are procured, ſuch the manner wherein they are removed from their native land, and wherein they are treated in our plantations. Thus far the Rev. John Weſley, chiefly from Benezet. ' *Cooper*, p 20.

" The average import of ſlaves into the European colonies may be 100,000, but theſe are only two-thirds of the import previous to the ſeaſoning, for one-third dies in the ſeaſoning, therefore, the actual import into the European colonies is at this rate 150,000   But this latter number is only four-fifths of the cargo when firſt laden, for one-fifth at leaſt dies in the paſſage, therefore the cargo when firſt laden was 180,000 men.   Moreover, it has been obſerved before, and proof has been offered ſufficient to eſtabliſh the fact, that for *one* man actually ſent down to the coaſt, at the very leaſt *four* were ſlaughtered   Hence *thouſands of people,* are annually murdered at the inſtigation of Europeans."

This ſtatement needs no comment. The moſt callous heart cannot reflect upon it without emotion, and every one who poſſeſſes a common degree of humanity is ready to imprecate the vengeance of Heaven upon the authors and abettors of ſuch unparalleled barbarity. What then muſt be his anguiſh on finding that he himſelf has, thoughtleſsly indeed, but really, been acceſſary to the crime, and is partaker in the guilt ? Yet, with regard to moſt of the inhabitants of this country, this is too ſurely the caſe.

For why is the Slave Trade carried on ? To ſupply the Weſt India planters with hands to cultivate the iſlands. And why are the iſlands cultivated ? To furniſh the inhabitants of Europe with ſugar*' If ſugar were not conſumed it would not be imported---if

---

* It is the cultivation of ſugar-cane alone which ſupports the trade, the other articles ſuch as cotton pimento, indigo, &c requiring comparatively little attention,

it were not imported, it would not be cultivated, if it were not cultivated there would be an end of the Slave Trade, so that the consumer of sugar is really the prime mover—the grand cause of all the horrible injustice which attends the capture, of all the shocking cruelty which accompanies the treatment of the wretched African Slaves.

If a person hire an assassin to destroy his enemy, both are justly considered equally guilty of the crime; and the case is precisely the same, if the first mentioned assassin procure a second, he a third, and so on to any given number; all concerned are, in the eye of reason and the law, partakers in the murder. And the criminality will remain the same, if the first instigator, and all the intermediate instruments, jointly attack their victim; the number concerned not altering the nature of the action. Yet should any be thought more guilty than the rest, it would certainly be the one, who by gifts or promises excited the others. Now let us apply this to the case in hand.

A number of persons offer a large sum of money for a certain natural production. The merchant is by this induced to import it, and the planter to cultivate it. But as the merchant will of course prefer the cheapest market, the planter must adopt the cheapest mode of cultivation, i.e. in the present case, must purchase slaves He, therefore, in his turn, offers a reward for *this commodity*, by which others are tempted to procure *it*, and, since it is not otherwise to be obtained, to procure it *by the annual* murder* of *many thousands of their fellow creatures.* The load of guilt bears equally upon every link of this infernal chain, upon every one who is either directly, or indirectly engaged in the cultivation or consumption of West Indian produce, but as in the case above stated, the first mover seemed more criminal than the rest, so, in this case, a larger portion of guilt may perhaps, not unjustly, be attributed to the consumer. The conclusion appears inevitable—may it suitably impress the heart of every reader.

---

* For knowingly to deprive a fellow creature of life, except in case of self-preservation, or in obedience to the sentence of the law, is most certainly, in a moral view, murder

Such is the nature of the African Slave Trade, and such the methods by which it may certainly be restrained, and in process of time annihilated. If the facts above stated are true, and the conclusions just, every person who habitually consumes one article of West Indian produce, raised by Slaves, *is guilty of the crime of murder*—every one who does it, when convinced that what has been said is true *is deliberately guilty*, and rendered more criminal by it being preceded by every species of cruelty and torture, which inventive barbarity can devise. Parents are dragged from their families, children from the arms of their parents, husbands and wives forced asunder, and hurried from a country dear to them as ours to us and led, through a life of unmerited calamity, to a violent or at least a premature death. And this not in small numbers—it is computed—reader stop and wonder, that ONE HUNDRED and EIGHTY MILLIONS* have already thus been sacrificed! What possible excuse can be offered for partaking of such accumulated guilt? Shall it be said that the abstinence of an individual can produce no effect? When a thousand musquets are levelled at an innocent bosom, is it no crime in me to direct another bullet at the victim? Nor is it sufficient to assert that the affair should be considered by our legislators—that it is their duty, not ours, to abolish the traffic—Let their sin be upon their own heads; does their guilt diminish ours? Shall we still purchase the fruit of fields cultivated at the expense of myriads of our fellow creatures, merely because the legislature has thought fit to license inhumanity —to sanction *murder*. Remember, friends, there is another tribunal, before which sooner or later we must all appear, the best of us will with reason tremble when that awful day approaches, but let it not be said, in addition to our other crimes, that we encouraged a traffic fatal to the happiness of so many of our brethren—of the

* The African Resident computes that at the time of his writing, nine millions of slaves had been consumed by the Europeans. Add one million at least since, for it is about ten years ago, 1787. Recollecting then that for one slave procured ten at least are slaughtered in a sudden onset, and a third in the seasoning and the unexaggerated computation will come out, that the infernal voracity of European avarice has been glutted with the murder of 180,000,000 of our fellow creatures. Cooper, p. 20.

children of that great Being, before whom we then shall stand.
Are our appetites so very much depraved, that we cannot relin-
quish one gratification, though called upon by the groans, and
tears of *millions?* Multitudes rejoiced when the Bastille fell, yet
how small the number there confined, how trifling the tortures
there inflicted, when compared with the numbers and sufferings
of the slaves, even on one plantation. But it is needless to en-
large—enough surely has been said to satisfy every one into whose
frame one atom of compassion enters, to interest even those who
though deaf to the claims of humanity shudder at the thought of
murder—to influence all who are in truth the disciples of that
master, who commands his followers to do to others, as they
would that others should do to them.

POSTSCRIPT.

The arguments by which those who continue to use West Indian
 commodities justify their conduct, seem principally the two
 following.

1. The object proposed in leaving off sugar is to procure the
abolition of the Slave Trade, but

(1) There is no reason to expect, that a number sufficient, in
any perceptible degree, to affect the consumption, will ever leave it
off; and

(2) If all the inhabitants of England were to leave it off, still the
demand from abroad is so great, that the trade would continue as
brisk as ever.

Answer. (1) The object proposed in leaving off sugar is to avoid
any share in the guilt of the most heinous crimes, and is equally
forceable whatever be the effect upon the Slave Trade. Because
theft and murder will still be committed, *may* I thieve and murder?

But 2 There is great reason to hope that the abolition of the
slave trade will be *thus* effected The number of those who ab-
stain from West Indian commodities, very rapidly increases, as
may be learnt by applying to the retail dealers. A considerable
grocer in Birmingham sells only half the quantity which he did

some months ago, and why should we suppose his case singular ? †
⌐ (3) Though, from accidental circumstances, the foreign demand may at present be considerable, what reason is there to expect
its continuance ? It is absurd to suppose that *others will begin* to
consume sugar, merely because *we cease*. Besides, why should
not the same arguments operate abroad, as at home ?

ii. There are many other commodities which are procured
by the commission of equal crimes, so many indeed, that in
the present corrupt state of society, it is impossible to avoid
contracting a similar guilt to that which is supposed to be
incurred by consuming sugar; it is inconsistent therefore, and
ridiculous, to leave-off that and continue the others.

Answer (1) This has been asserted, but not proved.

(2) That other articles ought to be relinquished, does not
prove that sugar ought not.

(3) There can be no grosser inconsistency than avowing a
regard to *humanity* and *liberty*, and at the same time encou-
raging a traffic *most fatal* to both.

(4) If the state of society be so corrupt that it is impossible
to avoid the commission of crimes equal to the slave trade,
it is high time that it should be altered and amended.

The papers have lately informed us that the slaves of St
Domingo have asserted, and in some measure recovered, their
native rights. And who knows but that their brethren in other
islands may be influenced by their example, and that the in-
famous traffic, which has been so obstinately persisted in, may
terminate in the expulsion of the West Indian Planters. There
is a point, beyond which, liberty, like air, cannot be com-
pressed, and it should be remembered that if ever it recovers
its elasticity, the violence and effect of the explosion will be
exactly proportionate to the force by which it hath been confined. Let slave-merchants and slave-masters tremble.

15 MA 56

† N B. I have just heard that numbers have left off sugar at Norwich and
Yarmouth, and that a grocer at Hackney has lost one third of his custom in this article. Anti-saccharine principles spread much in France.

CPSIA information can be obtained
at www.ICGtesting.com
Printed in the USA
BVHW011728160821
614506BV00013B/495